Volcanoes

David Lambert

Franklin Watts

London   New York   Toronto   Sydney

© 1985 Franklin Watts Ltd

First published in Great Britain
    1985 by
Franklin Watts Ltd
12a Golden Square
London W1

First published in the USA by
Franklin Watts Inc.
387 Park Avenue South
New York
N.Y. 10016

UK ISBN: 0 86313 274 X
US ISBN: 0-531-10009-X
Library of Congress Catalog Card
    Number: 85-50175

Illustrated by
Michael Roffe
Drawing Attention
Hayward Art Group

Photographs supplied by
Geoscience Features
Frank Lane Picture Agency

Designed and produced by
David Jefferis

Printed in Great Britain by
Cambus Litho, East Kilbride

Volcanoes

Contents

What is a volcano?

A volcano is formed when hot, melted rock from deep inside the Earth bursts through to the surface. This molten rock is called magma.

Volcanoes are found all over the world, both on land and in the sea. They start as holes or cracks in the Earth's outer layer, the crust. Hot magma and gases force their way up to the surface through these cracks.

Magma that flows from a volcano is called lava. Lava hardens as it cools. In time, erupting lava and ash may build a cone-shaped mountain with a crater at the top. There are many famous volcanic cones including Mt. Fuji in Japan and Vesuvius in Italy.

Volcanoes that erupt fairly often are called active volcanoes. Volcanoes that are non-active for many years between eruptions are dormant or "sleeping." Volcanoes that have stopped erupting are extinct.

▷ This cutaway view through the Earth shows a typical cone-shaped volcano.
1 Lava, gas and ash erupting from central cone.
2 Stream of molten lava flowing down the side of the volcano.
3 Magma forcing its way up through a central hole called a pipe.
4 Solid rock layers.
5 Magma chamber, deep underground.

Magma is *hot* – fifteen times hotter than boiling water – 2,732°F (1,500°C) or more. It often cools before reaching the surface.
Level sheets of solid magma underground are called sills; sloping sheets are called dykes.

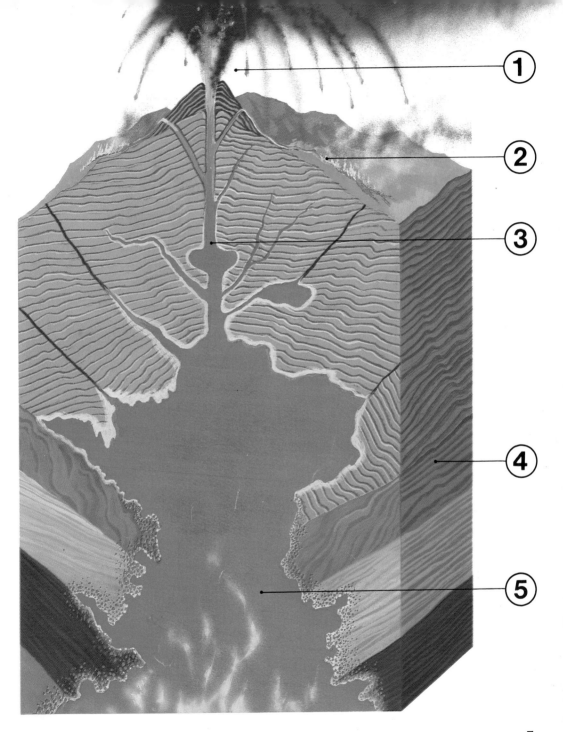

①

②

③

④

⑤

5

Mighty eruptions

Volcanoes erupt because of the way the Earth is made. Its hard, cool crust is a "jigsaw puzzle" of huge pieces called crustal plates. The lands we live in are all on these plates which move slowly. Below lies a thick, hot layer of rock called the mantle. In places this flows like syrup. Currents of molten mantle rise like heated water.

The picture below shows many of the places where volcanoes are found. Mid-ocean ridges are formed as rising

▽This cutaway view shows volcanic activity across a slice of planet Earth. Batholiths are huge blobs of once-molten rock. Iron-hard granite rock is an example of Batholith.

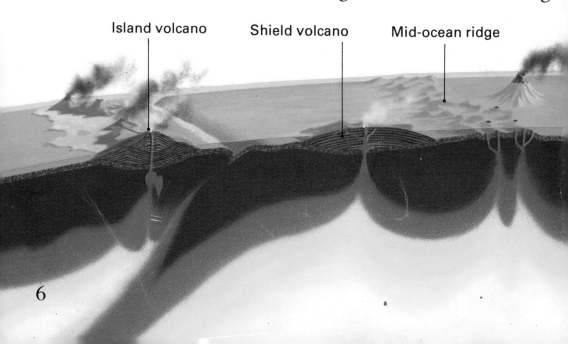

Island volcano   Shield volcano   Mid-ocean ridge

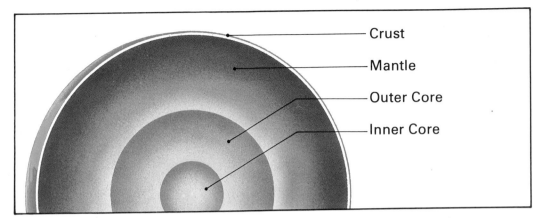

magma pulls crustal plates apart. Lava builds up to fill the gap and a ridge is formed.

A subduction zone is where plates collide. One plate is subducted, or drawn down, and melts. Some of the lighter melted rock erupts through weaknesses in the crust above.

△This diagram shows a cross-section through the Earth. Our world's interior is white-hot to within 124 miles (200 km) of the surface. The crust is like a cracked eggshell surrounding the hot insides.

Crust
Mantle
Outer Core
Inner Core

Subduction zone   Batholiths

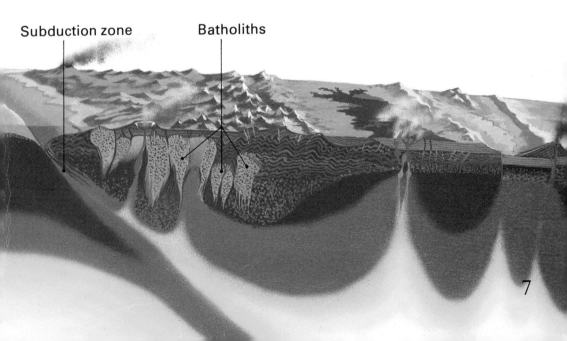

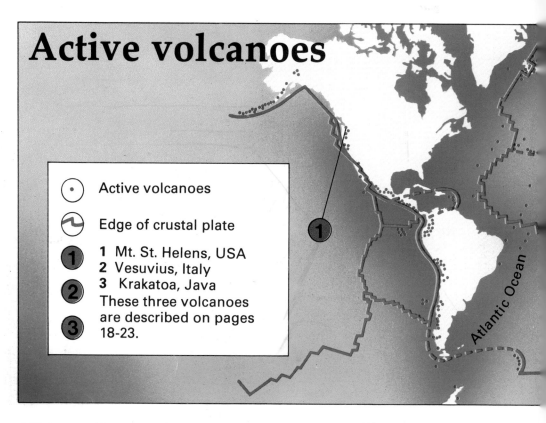

Active volcanoes

- ⊙ Active volcanoes
- 〰 Edge of crustal plate
- ① 1 Mt. St. Helens, USA
- ② 2 Vesuvius, Italy
- ③ 3 Krakatoa, Java
  These three volcanoes are described on pages 18-23.

Atlantic Ocean

△This map shows where most of the world's active volcanoes are. As you can see, many are at the edges of the huge drifting crustal plates.

We know at least 850 volcanoes have erupted in the last 2,000 years. Most of them have formed along the edges of crustal plates.

Colliding plates have produced volcanoes around the Pacific Ocean. People often call its rim the "Ring of Fire." Colliding plates also forced up the big Italian volcanoes Vesuvius and Etna.

Two separating plates caused the Mid-Atlantic Ridge that runs down the

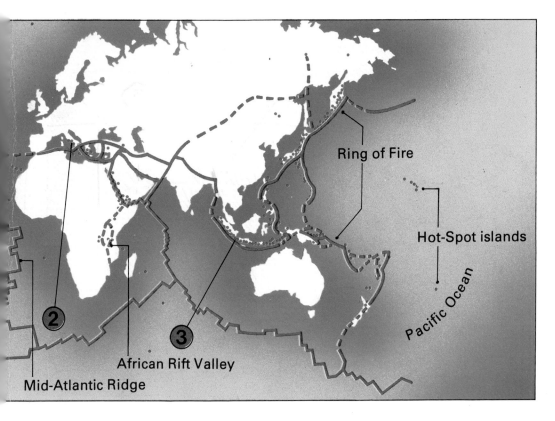

Ring of Fire

Hot-Spot islands

Pacific Ocean

2

3

African Rift Valley

Mid-Atlantic Ridge

middle of the Atlantic Ocean. As the plates slowly move apart, lava wells up to fill the gap between them.

In Africa's Rift Valley, volcanoes are rising where another crack is gradually opening. Many Pacific islands were formed, one by one, in rows above molten rock which was rising in the mantle. This rock burned holes through the crustal plate moving slowly above it.

△The crustal plates are all drifting in different directions. They move very slowly, only a few inches a year.

Underwater volcanoes

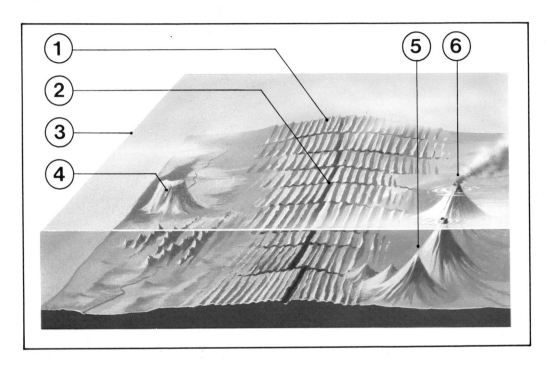

△Here you see a view of the volcanic underwater world.
1 Transform faults are cracks caused by jerky movements of separating plates.
2 Mid-ocean spreading ridge
3 Sea surface
4 Guyot
5 Seamount
6 Volcanic island

Thousands of volcanoes dot the bottoms of the seas. The Pacific Ocean alone contains about 10,000, although few are active at any one time.

Many rise hundreds of feet above deep underwater plains. These hidden peaks are called seamounts.

Guyots are "drowned" volcanoes with flat tops. Once they stood above the surface, but pounding waves wore away their cones. Some volcanoes sank

beneath the sea. These stood on ocean crust sliding into a deep trench, and down into the mantle.

Many undersea volcanoes form on the lava ridge that rises between separating crustal plates. The ridge's edges stick to the plates and become part of the ever–spreading ocean floor. The movement is often jerky, and faults or cracks form in the rock. You can see these faults on page 10.

△This picture was taken in 1963. It shows the eruption of a volcanic island, Surtsey, off the coast of Iceland. Iceland lies on top of the Mid-Atlantic Ridge and has many active volcanoes.

Rivers of fire

Quiet volcanoes belch out runny lava that flows far before hardening. These "basic" lava flows do not block craters which could bottle up explosive gases inside. As there is no trapped gas there will not be a loud bang. But small pockets of escaping gas can force up molten lava fountains. Stromboli in Italy is classed as a fairly quiet volcano. You can see it in the picture on the right.

Rivers of runny lava spill out from craters to build broad shield-shaped cones. Hawaii's shield volcano, Mauna Loa, is the broadest and highest mountain on Earth if its height is measured from the floor of the Pacific Ocean.

Lava flows also ooze from cracks called fissures. Some of this lava travels many miles before it cools enough to set and harden. The cooled lava forms sheets of basalt rock. Basalt covers much of Iceland, Northern Ireland, north-west USA and western India.

△Here you see a lava flow slowly engulfing an Icelandic town. This lava flow is cooling down and hardening. Other, hotter lava flows as fast as a river.

▷The picture shows the volcano Stromboli in Italy. This 1982 eruption is a *mild* one for Stromboli!

Bombs, dust and ash

△Heimaey, Iceland in 1973. The picture shows the early stages of a "fire fountain."

Many volcanoes make a loud noise when they explode. Most of them build steep cones of sticky acid lava. This lava quickly cools and hardens, and it sometimes blocks the pipe below the crater. The lava traps magma and hot gases such as sulfur dioxide and steam. In time, the pressure of gases blasts off the lava with a loud bang.

Pieces of lava soar into the air, harden and then fall as volcanic

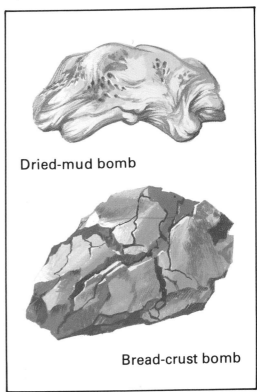

Dried-mud bomb

Bread-crust bomb

bombs. Smaller pieces drop as cinders. Tiny bits rain down as ash. Volcanic dust is blown high and far by the wind. Large amounts of dust can veil the sun to create spectacular sunsets and cause havoc with weather patterns.

A really huge explosion may blow the entire top off a volcanic cone and leave a vast crater called a caldera. One immense Japanese caldera measures 70 miles (112 km) around its rim.

△Some volcanic bombs look like lumps of dried mud. Others are shaped like crusty loaves of bread. Pieces of liquid lava that hit the ground build little spatter cones like the ones in Hawaii shown above left.

15

Hot springs and geysers

△Some life on Earth is very tough. The colors in these hot springs are caused by algae – organisms which thrive in these conditions.

◁A geyser erupts in Yellowstone National Park. Once an hour "Old Faithful" hurls near-boiling water as high as 197 ft (60 m).

Where volcanoes have been active, you often find hot springs and geysers. These occur in various places, including Iceland, New Zealand's North Island and Yellowstone National Park. Hot springs bubble up where hot rock has heated water underground. The water may be full of dissolved minerals. Some of these minerals cover the surface with crusts shaped as mounds or steps.

Geysers are fountains of scalding hot water that erupt from time to time. They spout where water fills natural pipes leading to deep chambers. Hot rock turns the water to steam. The steam blows the water in the pipe high in the air. Then cool water flows in to fill the pipe and chamber again.

Various gases and vapors spurt from holes or vents in or near volcanoes. These holes are called fumaroles or solfataras.

Vesuvius

△This is the shape of a man who was buried in the ash of the Vesuvius explosion. A plaster cast was made of the hole that his long-decayed body had left in the ash.

Terrible damage can occur if a volcano erupts without warning. This happened in southern Italy in AD 79.

No one knew when Mt. Vesuvius had last erupted. Farmers grew crops on its fertile slopes and two peaceful country towns – Pompeii and Herculaneum – lay nearby.

Suddenly Vesuvius poured clouds of scalding ash high into the sky. Lightning flashed as the sky darkened. Hot stones and rocks rained down and for days earthquakes shook the area.

The ash and poisonous gases made breathing difficult. Thousands of people left their homes and ran away. But thick ash quickly smothered Pompeii. The people still there choked in the ash

or suffocated from the poisonous gas.

Meanwhile a vast mudflow slid down from Vesuvius and literally buried Herculaneum.

Both towns were hidden and forgotten for hundreds of years. Then, in the 19th century, archaeologists started digging in the ruins of the disaster. Today you can walk through many of the ancient streets.

▽ This is what the scene could have looked like nearly 2,000 years ago in the coastal town of Pompeii.

Krakatoa!

△Red-hot volcanic bombs fell on the seas around Krakatoa. Boats that escaped the bombs were sunk by the *tsunami* and savage waters created by the explosions.

Late in the last century, Krakatoa exploded. It was perhaps the loudest sound ever made in the world.

Krakatoa was a volcanic island in what is now Indonesia. It had been quiet for centuries. Then, in 1883, ash clouds spurted out with loud bangs. These lasted for months and people on the nearby islands of Java and Sumatra got used to them. But, at last, sea water poured deep down into Krakatoa's magma chamber. The intense heat

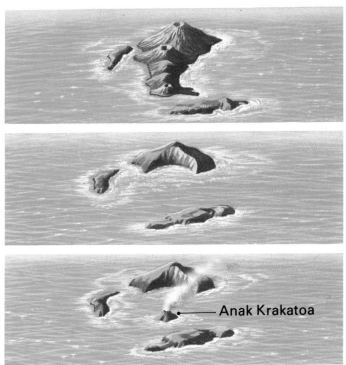

Anak Krakatoa

instantly turned the water to steam and the island blew apart with four immense explosions. The loudest bang was heard as far away as Rodriguez Island, 3,000 miles (4,800 km) away!

The explosions set off huge sea waves called *tsunami*. The waves roared over nearby islands and swamped far-off shorelines. Over 36,000 people were drowned in the disaster. After the explosion, two-thirds of Krakatoa had disappeared.

△The maps above show the island of Krakatoa.
1 Krakatoa before it exploded in 1883.
2 Krakatoa's remains soon after the explosion.
3 Krakatoa today. Anak Krakatoa – "Child of Krakatoa" – is a new volcano rising from the wreck of the old one.

Mount St. Helens

Snow-capped Mount St. Helens in the state of Washington had been dormant for 123 years. But gas pressure was slowly building up inside. Then, in 1980, came the biggest eruption in the USA for years.

Gas pressure blasted out the lava plug in Mount St. Helens' crater and

▽ Mount St. Helens looked like this before it erupted in 1980. Its top was a picturesque cone 9,667 ft (2,946 m) above sea level.

the volcano blew its top off.

A vast cloud of ash, dirt and rubble boiled into the sky. A wall of molten ash, gas and pumice (a light volcanic rock) swept down the northern slopes. Its scalding shock wave flattened forests and millions of river fish were boiled alive by the heat. Ash clogged the Columbia River and lay ankle-deep on roads and fields. Yet the death toll was lower than it might have been and most people escaped although over 60 people died.

▽The eruption blew the north side off Mount St. Helens. Its peak is about 1,300 ft (400 m) lower than before.

Predicting eruptions

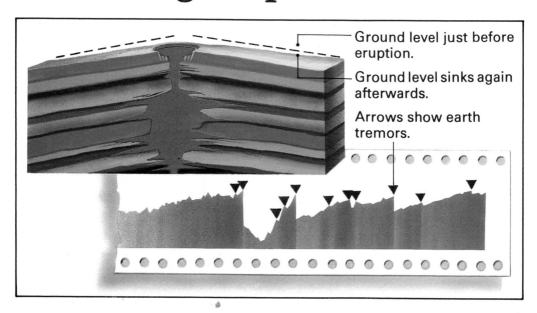

Ground level just before eruption.

Ground level sinks again afterwards.

Arrows show earth tremors.

△The cross-section above shows the principle of a tiltmeter. The ground rises with the swell of the magma underneath and this rise can be measured.
The chart is a seismograph trace – the "jiggles" show earth tremors.

Thousands of people live very near volcanoes. An unexpected eruption could endanger whole city populations. So various ways to detect earthquake and volcano activity have been devised.

Infrared photography can sometimes show the ground heating up. Some volcanoes give off chlorine and sulfur dioxide before erupting. They can be detected by sensitive "sniffer" equipment.

As magma rises inside a volcano, the

ground surface swells. The volcano may rise only a yard, but that shows up on instruments called tiltmeters. When Kilauea erupted on Hawaii in 1960, tiltmeters had given warning, so everyone nearby had time to get away.

Special instruments called seismographs record the tiny earthquake shocks produced by magma rising underground. Seismographs may record only six tremors a day on a quiet volcano, but just before an eruption this may rise to 600. No one can stop volcanoes erupting. But engineers can sometimes bomb or block a lava flow to make it change course.

△In this seismograph, a pen traces a wobbly line on a revolving sheet of graph paper.

▽Ash and lava buried this research laboratory on the slopes of Mt. Etna in Sicily. The volcano demolished the building during the eruption of 1971.

Useful volcanoes

▽ These substances formed in or with igneous, or "fiery," rocks, like those in a volcano.

Polished or cut gemstones like diamonds **4** and peridots **2** come from natural rock crystals **3**. Peridot is a form of the mineral, olivine **1**.
Borax **5** can be found in hot springs. Volcanoes give off steam **6** and sulfur **7**.

Volcanoes create as well as destroy. Their eruptions helped build the continents we live on. In the Pacific Ocean, many people live on volcanic islands.

Volcanoes have many uses in today's world. Crops grow well in rich volcanic soil. Glass and mortar contain sand obtained from the once-molten rock granite. Gold and tin are formed in molten rocks deep within the Earth.

Even electricity can come from power stations which use the heat from hot volcanic rocks.

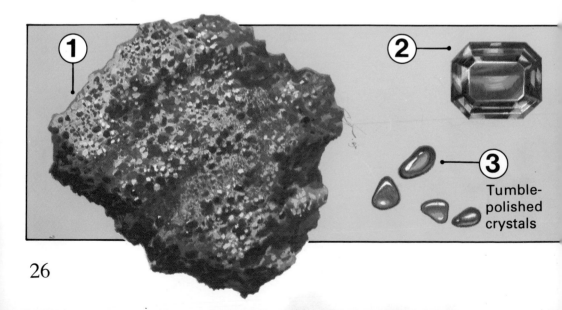

Tumble-polished crystals

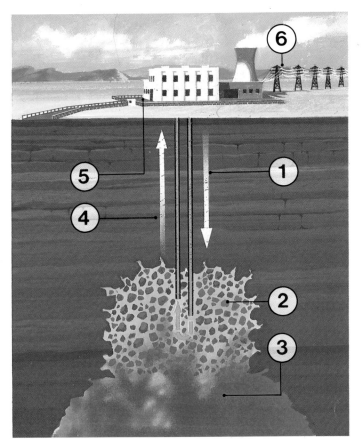

◁This picture shows how a power station can use hot rocks to make electricity.

1 Cold water pumped down to hot rock.
2 Rocks heated by magma.
3 Magma chamber.
4 Water turned to steam by heat, comes up another pipe system.
5 In the power station, steam is used to spin turbines which make electricity.
6 Cables carry electricity to a distant city.

Volcanoes in space

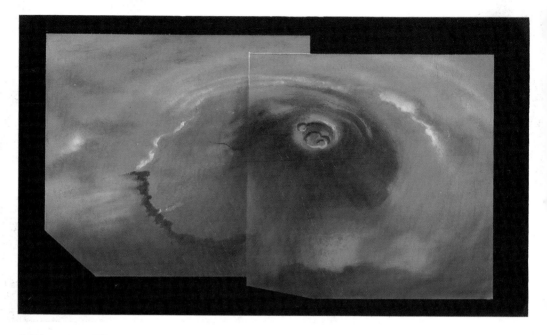

△Olympus Mons on Mars rises 14 miles (23 km) above the plains around. It seems to be a shield volcano like those of the Hawaiian Islands on Earth.

Earth is not the only world that has volcanoes. They can form on any moon or planet where molten rock punches its way through a cool, outer crust.

Spacecraft and radio-telescopes have shown us volcanoes on several moons and planets.

Mars has a group of four huge, very old volcanoes. Olympus Mons, the tallest, is probably the biggest volcano in the Solar System. But even larger vol-

canoes could lurk below the sulfuric-acid clouds of Venus. Radar measurements show one object 500 miles (800 km) across. It may be a massive shield volcano.

Our Moon's gray "seas" are old lava flows that leaked from fissures, or splits. The blister-shaped bumps are dome-shaped extinct volcanoes.

Young, active volcanoes erupt all the time on Io, a far-off moon orbiting the giant planet Jupiter.

△Io is a world of continuous volcanic activity. In this picture you can see a small volcano spraying out sulfur. The huge "moon" in the sky is the giant planet Jupiter. To scale against it, our Earth would measure barely ½ inch.

Glossary

Here are explanations of many of the technical words used in this book.

Acid lava
Sticky lava that cools and hardens before it flows very far. Acid lava builds up to create steep-sided cones.

Basic lava
Runny lava that flows far and quietly from craters or fissures. Basic lava builds shield volcanoes and wide sheets of lava and basalt rock.

Batholith
Giant blob of granite or other molten rock that has cooled and hardened underground.

Caldera
Huge crater formed when an explosive volcano blows its top off.

Crustal plate
One of the "jigsaw" pieces that make up the Earth's crust. Some carry continents, others form part of the ocean floors.

Dyke
Tilted sheet of magma that has pushed up through the rock layers. It cooled and hardened underground.

Explosive volcano
Steep-sided volcano that gives off acid lava, rich in gases. The volcano erupts explosively when high-pressure gases blow off the lava that has blocked its outlet pipe.

Geyser
Fountain of hot water squirting from a hole in the ground. The water is pushed up by steam, super-heated in an underground hot-rock chamber.

Guyot
Flat-topped undersea volcano.

Igneous rock
"Fiery" rock – any rock formed from molten magma.

Lava
Magma that has flowed out on the surface. It starts out hot and runny (or sticky) but cools off and hardens.

Magma
Molten underground rock. If magma escapes from a volcano it may form lava, ash, cinders or dust.

Pumice
Light volcanic rock, full of tiny holes that were made by various gases. Pumice is so light it will float in water.

Quiet volcano
Volcanic crater or fissure which erupts without a bang.

30

Fascinating Facts

Seamount
Underwater volcano.

Shield volcano
Volcano with gently sloping sides. Such volcanoes erupt quietly and give off much basic lava.

Sill
Level or nearly-level sheet of magma cooled and hardened underground.

Spreading ridge
Ridge of volcanic rock which rises to fill the gap between separating crustal plates.

Indonesia currently has 77 active volcanoes.

The longest lava flow oozed 300 miles (480 km) across North America 15 million years ago.

The highest volcano is the extinct Aconcagua in Argentina. Its peak stands 22,834 ft (6,690 m) above sea level.

About 1470 BC, the Greek island of Santorini blew up. The explosion is calculated to have been 120 times as powerful as the biggest H-bomb ever tested.

△This Hawaiian lava lake bubbles at an astonishing 2,012°F (1,100°C) – three times hotter than a baking oven.

The biggest known eruption of material came from Tambora in Indonesia in 1815. The volcano belched out about 20 cubic miles (80 cubic km) of dust, ash and gas.

Our word "volcano" comes from Vulcano Island off the coast of Italy. The Romans named it after Vulcanus, their god of fire.

31

Index